A Reproducible]
For Third Through Si:

Created by
Karen
Dickinson
and
Teresa Pahl

Scripture taken from the HOLY BIBLE,
NEW INTERNATIONAL VERSION®.
Copyright © 1973, 1978, 1984 by International Bible Society.
Used by permission of Zondervan Publishing House.
All rights reserved.

The "NIV" and "New International Version" trademarks
are registered in the United States Patent and Trademark Office
by International Bible Society.
Use of either trademark requires the permission of International Bible
Society.

Edited by Karen Brewer

The Standard Publishing Company, Cincinnati, Ohio
A division of Standex International Corporation

02 01 00 99 98 97 96 95   5 4 3 2 1

ISBN 0-7847-0329-9

To the Parent or Teacher:

God's Special Project—Me! is a creative write-in book designed to help third through sixth graders appreciate and celebrate their individuality and the uniqueness of God's plan for their lives, while developing their capacities for imagination and self-expression.

Each page introduces a thinking and writing project along with an idea for extending the journal theme with a special activity. The topics are arranged to enable students to complete one per week, from September through April. (In this way, the book may be finished in time for display at a springtime open house.)

Kids will enjoy building their faith and writing skills through *God's Special Project—Me!* Parents and teachers will find this book to be a valuable tool for motivating discussion, creative thinking and written expression, and for assisting students to actively apply Christian principles through writing and service projects.

Contents

God's Special Project—Me!
Special Delivery—The Day I Arrived   3
The Skin I'm In—The "Outside Me"   4
Another Look—The "Inside Me"   5
My Heart, My Treasure Chest   6
My Likes and Dislikes   7
The $100 Reward   8
Introducing . . . My Family   9
My Family Shield   10
If I Were Mom or Dad   11
A Special Person in My Life   12
A Recipe for a Friend   13
My Best Birthday   14
My Best Christmas   15
Three Wishes to Give Away   16
A Memo to Myself   17
    18

A Memorable Vacation
An Unforgettable Incident—
    Now I Can Laugh About It   19
My School   20
Some Special Books   21
This Is My Country   22
Dear President   23
Inside My Pet   24
How the Seasons Spice Up My Life   25
How I Spend 24 Hours   26
If I Had a Time Machine   27
My Very Own Invention   28
My Class Reunion   29
The Famous Future Me   30
A Letter From God   31
    32

"For we are God's workmanship, created in Christ Jesus to do good works,
which God prepared in advance for us to do" (Ephesians 2:10).

I am God's special project . . . a real one-of-a-kind! He knew me before I was born. He knows everything there is to know about me. Best of all, He loves me dearly.

God's plan for my life is unique . . . no one else has ever been, or ever will be, just like me. So how He works in and through me is something very special.

This book is about the person God made me to be . . . and the person He is helping me become!

Here's an Idea: When you do a special project described at the bottom of a page, if it is not one you give away, punch holes in it and keep it in a notebook in order with the journal pages.

Special Delivery—The Day I Arrived

Write a poem or paragraph about your birth and welcome into your family. Interview someone who can provide interesting details and your "vital statistics" (date, time, place, weight, length, etc.). Your parents, of course, are your best source!

"Your eyes saw my unformed body. All the days ordained for me were written in your book before one of them came to be" (Psalm 139:16).

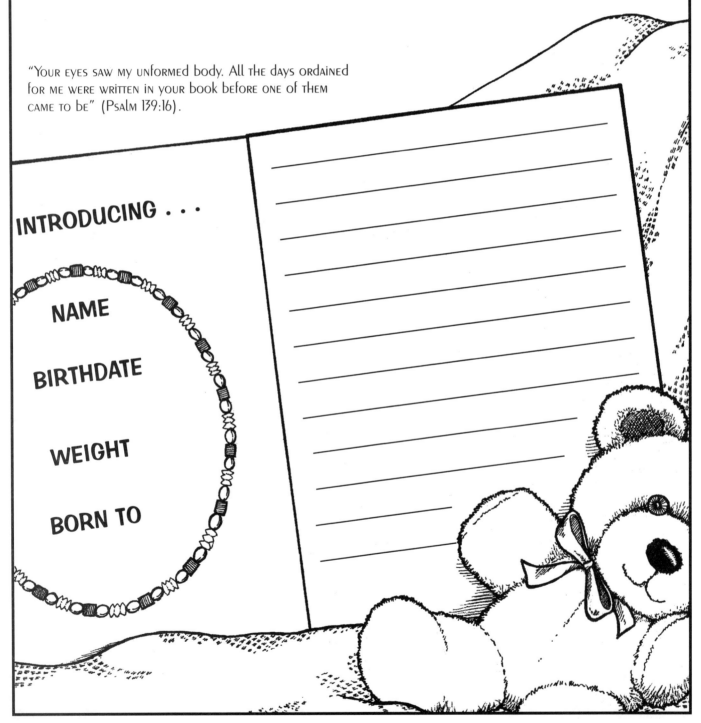

INTRODUCING . . .

NAME

BIRTHDATE

WEIGHT

BORN TO

Here's an Idea: Design a birth announcement for being born into God's family. What information might you include?

The Skin I'm In—The "Outside Me"

You are a masterpiece of God's design, an engineering marvel—your physique is unique! Write a physical description of yourself—what you see when you look into a mirror. Whether you compose a poem or a paragraph, be specific enough that someone could pick you out in a crowd, using only your written description to provide clues.

"I praise you because I am fearfully and wonderfully made;
your works are wonderful, I know that full well" (Psalm 139:14).

Here's an Idea: Help assemble a bulletin board display with photos and descriptions of classmates . . . without their names! Then enjoy trying to match them up.

Another Look – The "Inside Me"

The "inside you" is the person you are beneath your skin. It's the "you" known only to God and glimpsed only by those who are the closest to you. Describe the "inside you." Tell about your personality traits, talents, strengths and weaknesses, hobbies and interests, etc. God will use these raw materials as He begins to build and shape His unique plan for you.

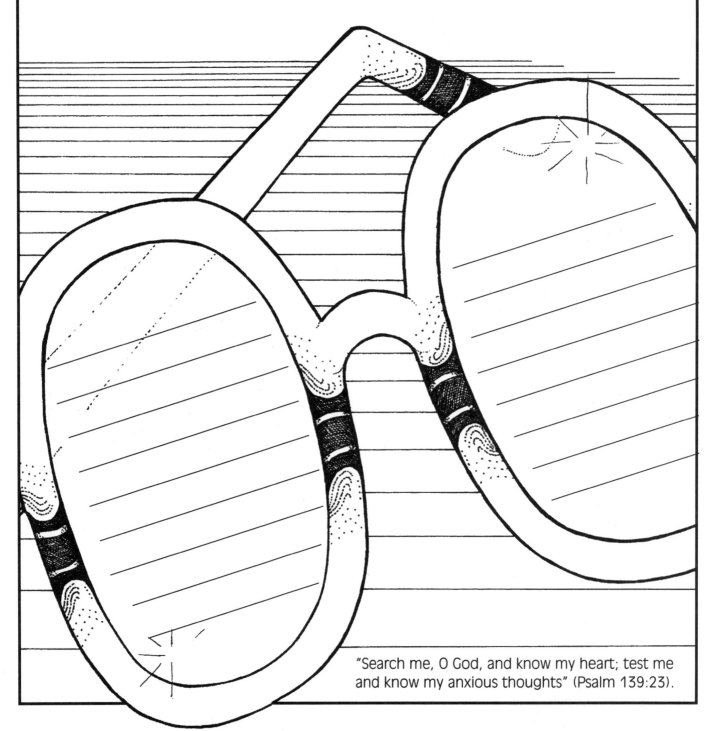

"Search me, O God, and know my heart; test me and know my anxious thoughts" (Psalm 139:23).

Here's an Idea: Make a collage of the "inside you." Cut out words and pictures from magazines to arrange and glue onto a sheet of your favorite color of construction paper.

My Heart, My Treasure Chest

Your "treasures" are people, things, even ideas that you value above all others. In Matthew 6:19-21, Jesus instructs us to choose our treasures carefully. Read the verses to see why. What do you value the most? This treasure chest represents your heart. Fill it up with words or pictures of people, things, and ideas that you prize.

"For where your treasure is, there your heart will be also" (Matthew 6:21).

Here's an Idea: Tell God how thankful you are for the treasures in your life. Present each to God in prayer, asking Him to help you be a good steward of each relationship, possession, or principle He has entrusted to you.

MY LIKES AND DISLIKES

God can use our tastes and interests in certain things, places, or activities to help give our lives a direction and as a basis for building relationships. As we grow, some of our tastes and interests may change, but God should always have first place in our lives.

List things, places, and activities (not people) that belong in these columns for you today.

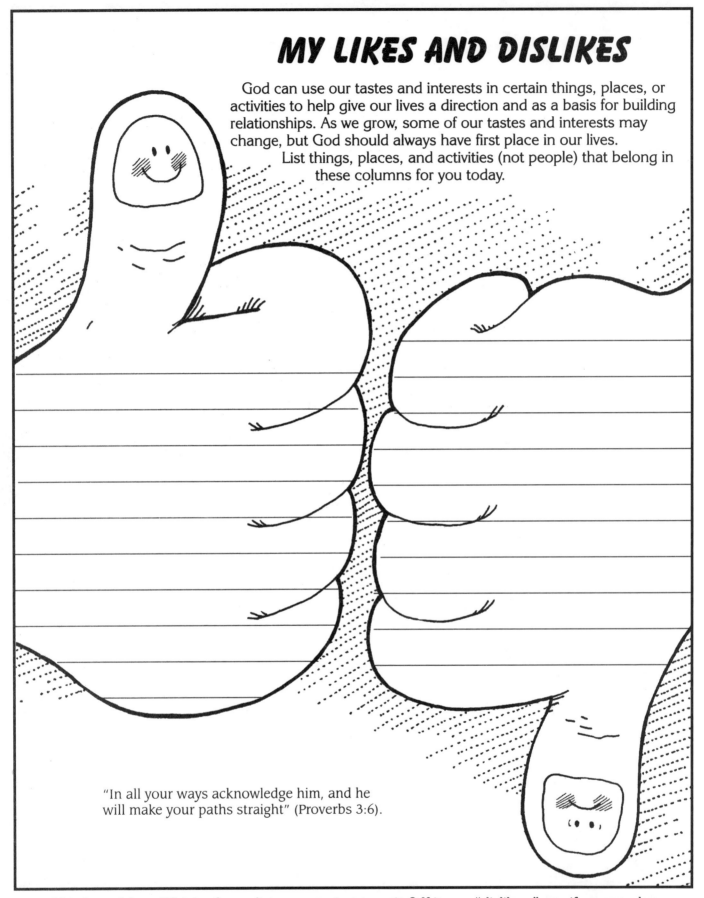

"In all your ways acknowledge him, and he will make your paths straight" (Proverbs 3:6).

Here's an Idea: Which of your lists was easiest to write? If it was "dislikes," see if you can be especially aware of good things in your life as you go through the rest of the day. Write a humorous poem based on one or both of your lists.

THE $100 REWARD

You find and return a lost wallet—just because you know it's the right thing to do and that it would bring honor to God. As an unexpected blessing, the grateful owner insists on rewarding you with $100! How would you spend the money?
Write your shopping list below.

"But seek first his kingdom and his righteousness, and all these things will be given to you as well" (Matthew 6:33).

SHOPPING LIST

ITEMS   **COST**

TOTAL $100.⁰⁰

Here's an Idea: Ask God for an opportunity to do a good deed secretly, so that no one could possibly know to reward you. Giving without any expectation of reward is exciting and may become habit-forming.

Introducing . . . My Family

Write a description of the family God gave you, telling a little about each person. Include names, ages, and their relationship to you. Tell about them "outside."

"One generation will commend your works to another;
they will tell of your mighty acts"
(Psalm 145:4).

Here's an Idea: Draw a picture of your family or mount a photograph of them on construction paper. Label and share your description and picture with your classmates.

My Family Shield

Design a shield depicting values and activities that are important to your family. Consider using colors (like blue for loyalty or white for purity) or animals (such as a lion for courage) as significant symbols. Add a family motto or Scripture verse if you can. Get your family's input if you would like to . . . and do share the results with them!

"His banner over me is love" (Song of Songs 2:4).

Here's an Idea: Make a large family shield for God's family. You might work with a group of friends as you develop your ideas. Share the result with your class, explaining the significance of the colors, symbols, and words you included.

IF I WERE MOM OR DAD

Your parents are the most important people God has placed in your life. Write about what they do that you hope to imitate when you become a parent. What might you like to do differently?

"'Honor your father and mother'—which is the first commandment with a promise—'that it may go well with you and that you may enjoy long life on the earth'" (Ephesians 6:2, 3).

Here's an Idea: Write a convincing essay explaining why your mom should be chosen as "Mother of the Year" or your dad as "Father of the Year." Leave your essay somewhere where your parent will find it!

A SPECIAL PERSON IN MY LIFE

Tell about someone who has been a special person God has brought into your life. It may be an older brother, an aunt, a grandparent, a minister, a neighbor . . . whoever comes to mind. Explain why this person is special to you. Then write down what you would like to say to God about this person.

"I thank my God every time I remember you" (Philippians 1:3).

Special Person Award

PRESENTED TO

_____

FOR

_____

_____

_____

_____

_____

_____

SIGNATURE

Here's an Idea: Make a card for your special person to let him or her know of your appreciation and admiration.

A Recipe for a Friend

Study several recipes to see how they are worded so that you can write an authentic-sounding recipe for a true friend. Under "Ingredients," you might include character qualities that make for strong friendships (such as 2 cups of loyalty) and activities that are fun to do with friends (such as 1 day of swimming). For "Directions" you will want to use recipe verbs such as *mix, blend, bake, etc.* to express other ideas that make friendships work (for example, *mix in* 1 neighborhood, gently *toss in* soccer practice).

How do you measure up to your own standards?
How do you measure up to God's recipe of a friend?

Recipe for _____
From _____
Ingredients _____ **Makes** _____

_____

_____

Directions _____

_____

_____

_____

_____

_____

"A friend loves at all times, and a brother is born for adversity" (Proverbs 17:17).

Here's an Idea: Now try your hand at developing recipes for other things—a happy family, your dog, the P. E. teacher, your little sister, a favorite Bible character.

MY BEST BIRTHDAY

Every new year is a gift from God. Write about your most memorable birthday. Include how old you were, who was there, and why this particular birthday was so special to you.

"Every good and perfect gift is from above, coming down from the Father of the heavenly lights, who does not change like shifting shadows" (James 1:17).

Here's an Idea: At Christmastime we celebrate Jesus' birth. What will you plan to do this year to make this an especially memorable birthday for Him? Talk it over with your family.

MY BEST CHRISTMAS

Write about your most memorable Christmas. Include how old you were, who was there, and why this particular Christmas stands out in your mind as special.

"Glory to God in the highest, and on earth peace to men on whom his favor rests" (Luke 2:14).

Here's an Idea: Taking the role of a Bethlehem shepherd, Mary, or Joseph, write about the first Christmas and the people, events, and emotions you experienced that made it so memorable.

Three Wishes to Give Away

In Psalm 37:4, God promises to grant the heart-desires of those who delight in Him. Suppose you were granted three wishes . . . but they must be used for other people—not for your own benefit. What would you wish for, and for whom?

"Now to him who is able to do immeasurably more than all we ask or imagine, according to his power that is at work within us, to him be glory" (Ephesians 3:20, 21).

Here's an Idea: Make a wish for each of your classmates. Share your wishes verbally or in writing. Might God be encouraging you to pray for a specific need in the life of someone you've been thinking about?

A Memo to Myself

God has already taught you some things that you want to be sure not to forget when you become an adult. Write a memo to yourself about it. Then resolve to keep this journal in a safe place so you'll have your reminder when you grow up!

"In his heart a man plans his course, but the Lord determines his steps" (Proverbs 16:9).

Here's an Idea: Have your family members write a few realistic goals for themselves for the coming year. Seal the goals in an envelope, put them in a safe place, and pray about them often. Check a year from now to see how far you have come in reaching your goals.

A MEMORABLE VACATION

Write about a special trip. Include when it took place, how old you were, where you went, and with whom. Describe what made this particular journey so special.

"I have come that they may have life, and have it to the full" (John 10:10).

Here's an Idea: Think about a Bible character who went on a memorable journey, like Abraham, Joseph, the Apostle Paul, Daniel, or Ruth. Put yourself in the character's shoes. Write about his or her journey as you did your own.

An Unforgettable Incident–
Now I Can Laugh About It

Write about an embarrassing or humorous incident that happened to you. How did you feel at the time? How do you feel about it now? How do you think God sees the situation?

"A cheerful heart is good medicine" (Proverbs 17:22).

Here's an Idea: Draw yourself as a cartoon character, living the incident you just described.

MY SCHOOL

Write about one or more of the topics listed below.

1) What I enjoy learning about most.
2) What I enjoy doing at recess or break times.
3) What skills I hope to improve on or grow in during this school year.
4) What are some of the special opportunities and challenges God is giving me this   year?

Aa Bb Cc Dd Ee Ff Gg Hh Ii Jj

"Instruct a wise man and he will be wiser still; teach a righteous man and he will add to his learning" (Proverbs 9:9).

Here's an Idea: Draw a map of your classroom, including the furniture. Label your desk and other significant locations in the room. Remember to thank God for this place and the people He has put here to help you grow.

SOME SPECIAL BOOKS

God wrote a special book for you—the Bible. Make sure you spend some time each day reading His Word and living by what it says.

Which is your all-time favorite fun-to read book, and why?

If you could write your own book, what would it be about?

"Finally, brothers, whatever is true, whatever is noble, whatever is right, whatever is pure, whatever is lovely, whatever is admirable—if anything is excellent or praiseworthy—think about such things" (Philippians 4:8).

Here's an Idea: Why not try to write your own book? Or at least, write a paragraph to begin it and one to end it. Has anyone written books on that topic before? If so, borrow one from the library and read it.

THIS IS MY COUNTRY

In what ways has God blessed this nation? Have you ever thought about that? If you were writing a letter to a foreign pen pal, trying to describe what is special and important about your country, what would you say? Write it below.

"Praise the Lord, all you nations; extol him, all you peoples. For great is his love toward us, and the faithfulness of the Lord endures forever. Praise the Lord" (Psalm 117:1, 2).

Here's an Idea: Writing letters gives us an opportunity God can use to touch someone else's life in a meaningful way. Consider corresponding regularly with a missionary, foreign student, or an out-of-town relative or friend.

Dear President

If you could write a letter to the President of the United States, what would you say? What might God want you to say? Write a two-paragraph letter. In the first paragraph, tell some things you appreciate about the President. In the second paragraph, tell some things you think the President should work on while in office.

"I urge, then, first of all, that requests, prayers, intercession and thanksgiving be made for everyone—for kings and all those in authority, that we may live peaceful and quiet lives in all godliness and holiness. This is good, and pleases God our Savior" (1 Timothy 2:1-3).

Here's an Idea: Recopy your letter neatly . . . and send it! Be sure to open with "Dear Mr., Mrs., or Ms." and close with "Respectfully yours." Address the envelope like this:

The Honorable (President's proper name)
President of the United States
The White House
1600 Pennsylvania Avenue
Washington, DC 20500

INSIDE MY PET

In Genesis, God gave man the responsibility of caring for His creation—and that includes animals. Do you own a pet? If not, what kind of pet would you like to own? Pretend to be that pet and tell your story—how you came to your owners, a typical day in your life, and some adventures you've had.

"Now the Lord God had formed out of the ground all the beasts of the field and all the birds of the air. He brought them to the man to see what he would name them; and whatever the man called each living creature, that was its name" (Genesis 2:19).

_____

_____

_____

_____

_____

_____

Here's an Idea: Draw your pet as a cartoon character dreaming about one of its adventures. Draw the adventure in a big "dream cloud" above its head.

How the Seasons Spice Up My Life

God's world is full of delights to enjoy. What are some favorite sights, sounds, smells, and sensations that you associate with each season? List them on the spice bottle labels below.

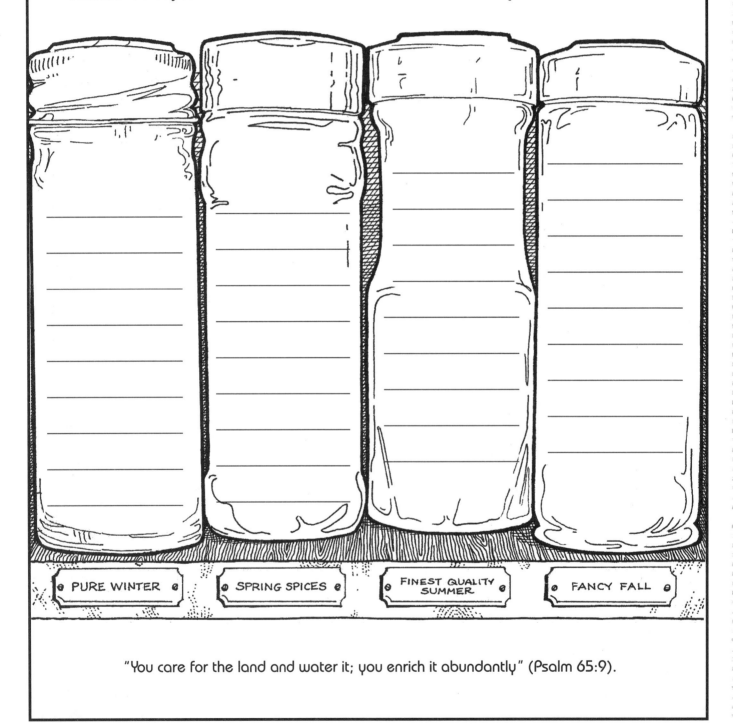

PURE WINTER   SPRING SPICES   FINEST QUALITY SUMMER   FANCY FALL

"You care for the land and water it; you enrich it abundantly" (Psalm 65:9).

Here's an Idea: Choose one of your lists to develop into a poem about the blessings of that season.

How I Spend 24 Hours

God gives us exactly 24 hours each day. He expects us to make wise choices about how we spend those hours. Write a list of weekday activities, in order, beginning with getting out of bed in the morning. Write down the approximate time each activity takes place for a full 24-hour day.

"There is a time for everything, and a season for every activity under heaven" (Ecclesiastes 3:1).

Here's an Idea: If your schedule does not usually include some time for personal prayer and Bible reading, find a logical spot for it and make a project of keeping that appointment every day for the next week.

If I Had a Time Machine

If you could travel back in time to meet a favorite Bible character or be on hand for a Bible story's original happening, whom or what would you choose to see? Write about your adventure.

"All Scripture is God-breathed and is useful for teaching, rebuking, correcting and training in righteousness, so that the man of God may be thoroughly equipped for every good work"
(2 Timothy 3:16, 17).

TIME · MACHINE

ON

OFF

DATE

PLACE

1
2
3
4

Here's an Idea: Illustrate your favorite Bible story, placing yourself in the picture where you think you would fit in had you actually been there.

MY VERY OWN INVENTION

Think of something useful you could invent that would benefit others. It could be a machine, a new game, or an improved process for making or learning something. Write a description or draw and label plans for your invention

Remember, God is the creator of the universe, and He made us in His image. So . . . our creativity and ingenuity come from Him!

_____

_____

_____

_____

_____

_____

_____

_____

_____

"Ah, Sovereign Lord, you have made the heavens and the earth by your great power and outstretched arm. Nothing is too hard for you" (Jeremiah 32:17).

Here's an Idea: Develop your invention plan further by making a model or a more detailed plan for it. Share it with your classmates in a commercial.

My Class Reunion

What if you and your classmates were to hold a reunion twenty-five years from now? How old would most of you be? _____ What year would it be? _____ Imagine such a fun gathering after all those years, then write about:

1) What your classmates are doing now.
2) Some things you will always remember about this school year.
3) Reasons to praise the Lord.

"Being confident of this, that he who began a good work in you will carry it on to completion until the day of Christ Jesus" (Philippians 1:6).

Reunion ?:00 p.m.

Here's an Idea: Stage a class reunion play towards the end of the school year. Have each person share his/her own ideas on the above topics to develop a script. Plan costuming and props, too! Perform it for open house, chapel, or another class.